LEADING
FROM THE
ROOTS

11 CHARACTERISTICS OF A GREAT LEADER

Nelson J. Estrada

Table of Contents

Introduction   5

What is a Leader?   10

Characteristic #1   21

Characteristic #2   26

Characteristic #3   31

Characteristic #4   37

Characteristic #5   41

Characteristic #6   47

Characteristic #7   53

Characteristic #8   57

Characteristic #9   61

Characteristic #10   65

Characteristic #11   69

In Conclusion   75

Introduction

Over the course of 36 years and several organizations, I have studied the topic of leadership. Now, when I say study, most people think I cracked open a few books and spent time dissecting them. That's only partly true. The other portion of my leadership study was experiencing it directly. My first experience in leadership started in 1st grade. Yes, 1st Grade. "Mrs. S" was my 1st Grade teacher. She would welcome us every morning when we walked in, she would have us all repeat a phrase to make sure we were paying attention and then she would begin teaching her class. "Mrs. S" made us feel special, in turn, we did anything she asked. In High School, it was "Mr. A", he was incredibly condescending and mean. He was cold when you walked in, you were beneath him. Your presence almost annoyed him, and because of this fear he instilled, we did anything he asked. Over the course of my life, I have experienced several leadership styles, from the autocratic dictator, to the laissez-faire *"que sera, sera"*. All of them serve a purpose, all of them belong somewhere.

The issue I realized I had with them is they were being used in the wrong places. Understanding what type of leadership is necessary in a particular situation is only part of the problem. Another issue we face in leadership is understanding we can be a leader at any level. I'm going to spend segments of this book mentioning leadership styles and what a leader actually is, but the majority of this book is discovering what makes a great leader. We are going to talk about what is at the *root* of every great leader, what characteristics that *root* produces, and most importantly, how to walk these characteristics out. As the old adage goes; "there's a negative to every positive". Nothing could be more true than this when it comes to leadership. In this book, we are also going to discover what is at the *root* of every bad leadership decision you've ever seen or heard of. The great thing is, no matter what bad decision you've ever seen or heard of, the *root* is always the same.

Now, this book may make you a little upset. This book may remind you of yourself or a leader you worked with in the past. This book is going to get you excited and optimistic, but it's also going to give you a bit of a reality check. I wrote this book to serve one purpose, and one purpose only, to help the development of great leaders in this world. What you will read in this book is nothing new. I didn't create new characteristics, I didn't create new words, what I did was identify "*11 Characteristics of a Great Leader*". What I mean by that is no matter what, no matter who and no matter how, you cannot be a great leader without these 11 characteristics. You may read this book and suggest more, fantastic! Feel free to add those to your personal list. But, I will promise you this, you cannot remove a single-one of these 11 and still be considered a great leader. These 11 characteristics are going to challenge you, stretch you, make you uncomfortable and push you to the limit of your capacity…and that's a great thing! Don't resist the feeling of growth as you go through this book, don't decide to skip a characteristic, because you feel like you've "arrived" at this one. See this process all the way through and you will see a dramatic, positive change to your leadership.

As I ask all my clients, *would you bet the future success of your business, family or relationships on the leader you are today*? If the answer is anything other than an astounding *yes*, then keep reading. Most people, if they were being honest with themselves, would say *no* to that question. Why? Because we all have room to improve in the area of leadership. Leadership is an on-going process of development. Leaders never stop growing, learning or developing. This is a life-long process of mastery. In order for you to know what makes a great leader, it's important to debunk and eliminate the myths that has followed this important role in your life. It's important to identify the lies we are telling ourselves that make a leader.

We have been misinformed, misled and we have misunderstood what makes a leader. There are too many people walking around with the capacity to be a great leader but don't see themselves as one, due to the misconception of leadership. Today, we are going to end that once and for all.

My biggest passion and desire is to see you successful in your leadership. I have seen so many people go on in their everyday lives, missing the chance to impact another with their leadership, all because they simply didn't view themselves as a leader. I have seen people promoted to positions of authoritative influence, but failed, because the position they were in required a leader, not a manager. I have seen organizations move or pass on a great leader because the other candidate had more time on a job, thus resulting in a cultural mess on the team they were leading. I have seen ministries fall apart at the hands of a great person, but an ill-equipped leader. Understand that if you have failed as a leader, it does not make you a bad person. You are not identified by your mistakes, rather your attempts to learn from them. Anyone can be a great leader, but not everyone will attempt to acknowledge their short-comings.

Whether you are the *President of the United States of America*, or the person who organizes your weekly book club, leadership is required and expected from someone in that group. For many, leadership is an intimidating subject. With the word 'leadership' comes a certain internal expectancy. We tend to characterize ourselves as 'unqualified' because of the mistakes we've made or the flaws we have. Don't fret, you're in great company! Everyone has them! I truly believe this book is designed to equip you with the necessary tools to address any flaw you have or mistake you've made, to 'qualify' you for your role as a leader. Make no mistake about it, there is an expectant behavior when it comes to leadership. This book is going to help you get there.

If you can master these 11 characteristics, you can be a great leader. It's going to require time, energy, effort, patience, accountability and a passion to be a great leader. If you can commit to those 6 things, then you are half-way there! Leadership development is a 'crock-pot', not a 'microwave'. This will not happen overnight, people won't see you as a leader because you committed 30 days to reading a book and testing out the 11 characteristics. People will view you as a leader when the actions match the words over an extended period of time. People expect a considerable amount of growth in a considerable amount of time. Let's go to work!

What is a Leader?

If you took the time to recount everyone who was influential in your life, that you viewed as a leader, my guess is that most of them are probably in a position of authority. When I say 'leader', I would venture to guess your mind takes you back to someone who made you feel good and made you excited to take-action. I would also venture to guess they were a Teacher, President, Boss or Parent. You subconsciously, viewed them as 'above you' in rank. If so, that's a pretty standard thought behind the word 'leadership'. Our whole lives we have been trained and led to believe that leadership had to do with a title in an organization or position in a social group. However, we can find a leader anywhere! The person who made you feel good and excited to take-action, isn't a leader because of the position they were in, but rather because of how they made you feel. They had a *positive* influence on you to achieve a common goal. That's what made them a leader, and that can be found anywhere. *Positions give you power, leaders give you purpose*!

There's a reason we look at someone in a position of authority and instantly give them a certain level of influence on us right away. We have been designed to think that their position equates to leadership. You can always *see* when power walks in the room, but you can *feel* when a leader does. Sometimes, we can mistake the two. Rear Admiral *Grace Murray Hopper* stated so eloquently, "You manage things; you lead people". Leadership isn't a position or a title, it's not a spot on an organizational chart. Leadership doesn't mean the louder voice or the person who has the authority to control something. Leadership doesn't mean automatic buy-in either (we will circle back to that a little later). Leadership is the person who can have the *positive* influence on the organization. You are going to hear the word *organization* a lot in this book. When I say *organization*, I don't necessarily mean a business or company (although I will in most instances), for the sake of this book, we are going to identify the word *organization* as two or more people in a group.

Good at What I Do, Not Who I lead

When I was young and under-developed in my leadership, I was promoted to a position of authority as Branch Manager of a bank. I was highly ambitious and ready to take on the world of banking. I had just left a role as a Business Banker where I was rather successful in my sales and made a decent name for myself. Prior to that, I did very well on the consumer side of banking. I felt like my promotion to branch management validated me and people recognized I was awesome (do you see the incredible cliff I was approaching). The one thing I will say I had going for myself was that I wanted to see my new team succeed. I wanted to see them hit their sales goals, get bonus checks and make good money…my way. Here I was, this young 20-something year old with a clear vision on how things were going to be done and what we were going to see. Anything outside of what I taught them was a complete load of garbage and it wouldn't work. I was the *alpha* and *omega* of branch management. Watch out!

From day one, I had people on my team in tears and in fear. I had no idea why they were crying and what they were scared of. I was here to make them more money than they ever had before. What was the problem? What I didn't realize as a young leader, was that I hadn't even got the buy-in of my team before I started talking about where we were heading and how we were going to do it (my way). You mean to tell me my title didn't make them automatically get behind what I was saying, and be just as excited as I was? Now, in hindsight, I looked like a complete idiot. Although my intentions were to make them successful, I assumed that my title made me their 'leader'. Let me be first to tell you, I was wrong. Really wrong. Leadership wasn't in my position, leadership was in my ability to *positively* influence my team reach a common goal. That was going to take much more than a title.

The Risk of the Myth

The myth that leadership is a title can be incredibly bad for your success as a leader. To believe that leadership is a title, positions you in a place of vulnerability, but not in the good way. You are vulnerable to lose key contributors on your team, due to your arrogance. You are vulnerable to fail on the interpersonal level, missing the critical connection every leader needs with their team, due to your naivety. You are vulnerable to fake loyalty, only until the next opportunity presents itself, due to your lack of caring for your team. *Titles establish structure, leaders establish relationships.* We don't neglect the former for the latter, but we certainly don't sacrifice the latter for anything.

The organizational chart in every company establishes the power, but the influence is inter-woven with people like you, all throughout that chart. There is not one person that is responsible for the success of many. Teams are brought together and inspired by leadership, but it is a collaborative effort for them to be successful. Positions of authority can set you up to have even more influence, because of your position. However, if you aren't ready to sit in the chair, it can expose your inadequacy in a way you could never imagine.

So, let's be clear, leadership is not position or title. Authority does not mean you're a leader, it simply means you're in charge, and that's not always good. *Leadership is your ability to positively influence action, demonstrate character and build trust in your team to reach a common goal.* If I can urge you to do anything in this chapter, it's to highlight, underline, maybe even tattoo that last sentence. There are several key words in that sentence that (if studied) will remind you of what is missing when you feel like you are failing as a leader. Let's dissect it a little bit.

Ability

Let's start with the word *ability*. Leaders are *able* to…well…lead. If you are in a position where you don't feel like you can lead, but you are the person required to lead, it's a good time to pause and do a little self-analysis. Maybe you aren't the person for the role right now? Maybe you have some personal things to work out before you put yourself in this level of influence? The leader has to feel *able* enough to lead the group, or they shouldn't do it. Trying to lead when you don't have the *ability* is selfish. That selfishness is only going to lead to failure for you and the team. Make sure you feel *able*.

Positively

The second word we are going to dive into is *positively*. If I were to simply have left off the word *positively*, we could have assumed influence would be sufficient. History shows us that's not always the case. There have been many 'leaders' who have 'influenced' people to action for a common goal. World War II, at the foundation, was started by a leader who influenced a nation to action for a common goal. Germany believed what they were doing was right and that the rest of the world was wrong. Places like Zimbabwe and Uganda have both experienced what it is like to be under the influence of a leader who is aiming toward a common goal of his/her team. You might think this is a bit over-the-top and extreme, but we can't overlook the importance of the word *positive*. Every one of those leaders started with influence and a goal. But at the core of the problem was their character. *Positive* influence is a game-changer for leadership. It shifts the pendulum to a clear-cut direction. It isn't broad or manipulative, we know it is going to be *positive*, not just influential.

Influence

The third word we are going to address is *influence*. You have to take the time to ask yourself; *"Do I have influence on this team?"* If the answer is *no*, maybe this isn't your time. That has nothing to do with who you are personally; it simply means you are lacking in one of the 11 characteristics we are going to address later on. Now maybe you're saying, "Nelson, I am the CEO, I can't step aside and just work on a characteristic. There is a business to run here." That's false. To be quite frank, you can't afford not to. Remember the question I asked earlier? *Would you bet the future success of your business, family or relationships on the leader you are today?* That is exactly what you're doing when you don't take the time to step aside and work on that characteristic. As the CEO, you should have been building up future leaders under you who can step into your role for a short period of time. You don't have to disappear from the organization. You simply have to remove yourself from the responsibilities to address the character of who you are. That level of honesty will do wonders for your influence later on. *Don't let your pride be your guide.*

Action

Fourthly, let's talk about *action*. In the words of the

legendary Running Back Marshawn Lynch, "I'm bout that action boss." There is a plethora of colloquialisms that align with Marshawn Lynch's wisdom. From 'talk is cheap' to 'the proof is in the puddin'', We all know that 'actions speak louder than words' (I can go all day on this). *People are heard by the words and felt by their actions.* As a leader, it is your job to make people feel what you're saying. Action moves people. When your team sees you act, they react, by mimicking your action (again, get the highlighter out). People have to see you in action! Nothing is more respectable than seeing your leader roll up their sleeves and do something they've asked their team to do. A leader once told me; "If serving is beneath you, leading is above you".

Demonstrate Character

The fifth part of this definition of leadership I'd like to address is the phrase *demonstrate character*. In every great leader, there are 11 core characteristics. These 11 core characteristics aren't necessarily displayed all the time, but they should definitely be displayed. This is different than action, as action is something you would display physically. In displaying action, you would be first on the conference call, or first in the office. Maybe you jump in a strategy session on a team that reports to you, to help guide the conversation? Maybe you don't just organize your book club, but you help bring food as well? Whatever the action is, it's always physical. Demonstrating character is a little more elusive. Let's say you're the Senior Vice President of an organization and the CEO comes to acknowledge the wonderful effort you put in to achieve your goal. An SVP that lacks humility might say something like; "Thank you sir! I worked really hard this quarter to reach that pinnacle. I really appreciate your compliment." Although you were the leader who had the *ability to positively influence action* to *reach a common goal,* you weren't the sole reason for the success of the team. An SVP who is humble might say something along the lines of; "Thank you sir! This team really worked hard this quarter and gave it all they had. I really appreciate their effort and I could have never done it without them." There is a monumental difference between the two and you were able to *demonstrate character.*

Build Trust

Lastly, and maybe most importantly, I'd like to talk about how to *build trust.* I shared a personal horror story about my first real leadership experience at the beginning of this chapter. It was a lesson of many, but one of the lessons was about building trust. Trust is a very hard thing to build, and a very easy thing to lose. But trust doesn't have to be a fine line, if you don't want it to be. You can establish clear-cut boundaries for yourself that will prevent you from ever crossing the line and breaking the trust of your team. However, I'd like to first discuss how to build the trust. If you follow, sequentially, the break-down order that I just laid out for you, you will be well on your way to building trust.

Trust is a compounding series of displayed actions that lead a person to believe in who you are, to a point where they will allow you to guide them in a direction you'd like to take them. Notice I didn't say anything about words. Words are meaningless in trust, without the display of actions. If you are able to positively influence action, you in turn will have your chance to demonstrate a character that builds trust. If you fail to positively influence action, your character demonstration won't move anyone and you in turn will not build a trust to lead this team anywhere. Why? Because you are lacking influence. If you have the influence, but lack the demonstration of character, you certainly will never build trust.

All these steps work sequentially and collectively. This definition of leadership alone, is a big pill to swallow. This explanation of leadership defies the very understanding we have been taught to understand. Yet, our experiences of poor leadership intuitively told us; "something is wrong". The reason why a leader has inspired us or disappointed us is not because of the position they've held, but because of the character of who they are. So, if leadership is not a position or place on an organizational chart, and it is in fact about your ability to positively influence action, demonstrate character and build trust in your team…where does all that begin?

Identifying the Bad Fruit

As much as I want to answer that right now for you, there's a few things we need to be able to identify, to fully understand where we currently lie in our leadership. Every poor decision made by a leader is *rooted* in something. These decisions aren't made on a whim; they are made based on the *root* of the leader and the characteristics they *currently* possess. When it comes to poor leadership, there are several *red flags* you are almost guaranteed to see in all of them. In a poor leader, you are going to see the following characteristics: pride, arrogance, blind to flaws, indecisive, non-attentive, detached, unaware and they will be "I" or "Me" driven. No matter the person, if they are a poor leader, you will see one or several of those characteristics. It is inevitable. I even challenge you to think back to a poor leadership experience in your life and find whether or not any of these characteristics surfaced.

These "bad fruit" characteristics are all related to the *root* of that leader. You may read that list and think, "this is a bad person", but honestly, they're not. They are just *rooted* in the wrong characteristic. The *root* of this leader isn't bad, it's insufficient. *The root of every bad leader we've ever seen is insufficiency.* This person falls short of expectations and lacks an adequate supply of the proper characteristics of a great leader. This doesn't make this person bad, as much as it makes them unaware of what it is they are missing (which is one of the "bad fruits" on this tree).

Poor leadership is nothing new, it is documented as early as King David, sleeping with one of his soldier's wife and having that soldier killed at war to cover it up. Poor leadership has been around for thousands of years. Just like King David, the *root* of every poor leadership decision is a state of being *insufficient*. The concept of leadership cannot be suppressed down to the idea that it is simply a position. Leadership is everything for us, yet nothing without us. Leadership must be respected for its infinite value on the lives of ourselves and others. Let's make sure we treat it with care by identifying and developing the *11 Characteristics of a Great Leader.*

Characteristic #1

In our current day, a lot of emphasis has been placed on social media. How we market products and services, how we get new "friends", and even how we "connect" with others. One thing I absolutely refuse to do in the social media era, or in any text form for that matter, is build relationships with my team. I placed too much importance on face-to-face time, to leave it subject to a social media post. I love spending quality time with people, getting to know them, hear their concerns and listen to them speak. One of the 11 characteristics every leader must possess to be great is the ability to be a *listener*. Listening to the people in your organization is invaluable to your success and theirs.

I remember sitting down one day to have coffee with someone I looked up to. I was so excited that the day before I wrote down questions, picked out the right outfit and even got a fresh haircut. I wasn't sure what I was looking to accomplish with my hair and wardrobe, but it just felt appropriate. I met him at a local coffee shop near his office. He walked in, I had a huge smile on my face, and I was ready to pick his brain. I was fully prepared to write down anything and everything he said. He greeted me warmly, sat down at the table and ask me, "Nelson, how are you doing?" We were off to a great start. I offered to buy him a coffee and we began to talk. His phone went off and that was just about the end of our conversation. From that moment on, I couldn't get his attention. I'd ask him questions, pen in hand, ready to write. He would begin a sentence, stop talking, apologize for being in his phone and continue to do so anyways. I was so frustrated that I put so much energy into preparing for this meeting, just to be ignored. I even asked if he needed a minute to handle something important, he stated he didn't.

At that point, I assumed he would get the hint. Nothing. With no hesitation, he hopped right back to his texting and intermittent conversation. This is the exact feeling of every single person on your team, in your organization or in your personal life, when you are not present with the one in front of you. *Great leaders respect the people in front of them.* Nothing is more important than the undivided attention of the person sitting across from you. As a leader, we need to be present, or don't begin your meeting until you can be. Your presence has significant value to those you lead. Whether it be those in your home, your personal circle or your business, they care about your presence. Honor them with it.

Silence is Golden

Another component of being a great listener is being quiet. There's a saying I heard once; "God gave us two ears and one mouth for a reason." *Great leaders are great listeners.* Listening requires your undivided attention and silence. People are meeting with you because they have something to say, let them say it. Leadership isn't about controlling people. It is about having a countenance and a posture of attentiveness. You might wonder what that looks like, if you're someone who is insufficient in this characteristic. Let's explore that a little bit. Have you ever been talking to someone and you generated a response in your head before they finished their sentence? Ok, maybe not you…but you know a guy. That is the exact opposite of what it looks like to be a great listener. Listeners take the time to let the other person finish talking. They recap what they heard for clarity. They don't fire off responses just because they have something great to say, or because they have the answer and they don't need to hear the rest. It's not about having the answer, as much as it is having respect for the person on your team or in your life.

R-E-S-P-E-C-T

Navigating a conversation with someone on your team can be challenging at times. Sometimes what you are navigating is a difference of opinion that needs to be heard from both parties. The important thing to understand here is that you are responsible for you. If you have a difference of opinion that's fine, but as the leader in order to be great, you have to respect their ideas. This isn't about surrendering your own, this is simply about making you a better listener.

When you lack respect for someone else's ideas, your ears tend to shut off and your mind begins to prepare its response. Avoid that at all costs. When you allow yourself to listen clearly and focus on the person in front of you, you avoid another major pitfall in listening. It's a trigger for many called sarcasm. Part of being a great listener is responding adequately, based on the information you just diligently listened to. Obviously, your conversations with your team are not going to be monologues. They're going to be dialogues. In order for you to have an effective conversation, you have to avoid sarcasm. Sarcasm weakens you as a leader. It tells the other person you lack the intelligence to hear a difference, and still be able to articulate yours.

Having the courage to sit down with a leader can be difficult for many people. It can be so difficult at times that it's downright frightening. This is also known as *Pistanthrophobia*, or the fear of trusting someone. Over 15 million Americans are affected by this phobia. Remember, as a leader, you are sitting down with someone who is being vulnerable with you. Leaders have the ability to positively influence people's lives with every interaction, you also have the ability to influence their life in the worst way possible. Don't underestimate just how much influence you really have on that person.

When someone has decided to open-up to a leader and be vulnerable, they are literally saying that have so much respect for who you are and what you do, they are willing to share with you their inner most feelings. Whether it's an opinion on a new policy, or an issue they are struggling with, they have chosen you to share that with. Listening is a learned skill, which means you're going to have to intentionally practice this. There is no better group to practice it with than your organization or personal relationships. Make yourself accountable by letting a few of them know your goal to be a great *listener*. Ask them how you could have done better. Allow yourself to be vulnerable with your team. This level of transparency creates channels of trust with your team. Remember, building trust is part what it means to be a great leader. *Be a great leader by being a great listener.*

Characteristic #2

If you spent any time volunteering in church, you are quickly introduced to filling more than the role you signed up for. It is just part of church culture. When you have a flexible, talented team member, you use them in several roles. Now this isn't always the best idea, as burnout happens quick; but it isn't so much about filling a role as it is increasing their capacity. In many churches, the hardest roles to fill are on the stage. It's hard to find someone who can get on a stage and draw in an audience with their words.

Maybe you want to rotate some servant leaders on stage to provide the offering message, or the announcements for the week, but finding one that can articulate it is a challenge. In leadership, even if it's not on a stage, it's no different. In order for anyone to be a great leader, they have to be a great *communicator*. You might read that and think; "I can get away with being a great leader, without being a great communicator." I'm sorry, but that is simply not true.

Be Prepared

Leadership requires communication. Being a great communicator can be intimate (one on one) or be formal and public. When you're a leader, communication is a key component to your success. There are several steps to being a great communicator, that will ensure you are appreciated and respected as a leader. One of the key elements of being a great communicator is to *prepare before you present*. Seattle Seahawks Quarterback, Russell Wilson says, "The separation is in the preparation." Russell is spot on! What separates a great leader from one who is insufficient in their communication, is one who is prepared. When you prepare for your talk with your team, whether it be a staff meeting or an annual conference, preparation is necessary for clarity.

Being prepared before you communicate ensures you are going to get the critical pieces of your message across to your team. It's hard for your team to listen to you, let alone follow what you're saying, when you're a bad communicator. This lack of clarity brings many issues to the surface such as; missed deadlines, overspending, misdirection, wastes of time and additional communication (usually resulting in the leader thinking the team member is incompetent). *Miscommunication is missed opportunity for a leader.*

Be Concise

In order for a great leader to be a great communicator, the leader must prepare and keep their message *concise. Great leaders understand the power in the right words, not many words*. According, to *Microsoft Corp.*, the attention span of the average adult is 8 seconds. I will repeat that. According, to *Microsoft Corp.*, the attention span of the average adult is 8 seconds. This is highly due to our heavily digitally enhanced lifestyle. It doesn't take a lot of words to get your point across, it takes the right words, the right way, at the right time. Trying to keep the attention of your team because you think the more you talk, the more they'll listen, is counter-productive to what you're actually trying to accomplish. Being concise in your communication allows for your team to receive, analyze, interpret and apply the information you are providing. No one enjoys drinking water from a firehose.

Stay on Track

Another component of being a great communicator is the ability to *stay on track*. In 2009, Disney's Pixar came out with a movie entitled; "Up". In the movie "Up", there is a talking dog named "Dug". "Dug" was a happy, polite, well-mannered dog. However, one of the issues he had was that he couldn't stay on track when he was talking. Periodically, in mid-conversation "Dug" would yell out; "Squirrel!" Apparently, squirrels were able to throw "Dug" off track and grab his attention. Leaders who are insufficient in their communication are "Dug-ish". Staying on track when you are communicating with your team, is an important facet to you being a great communicator. It is nearly impossible, as the listener, to stay interested in what anyone is trying to say when they are all over the place. Don't let the "squirrels" take you off track, in a direction that loses your teams focus. *Prepare before you present* what you are going to say, *keep it concise* and *stay on track.*

Make Eye Contact

One of the hardest things for me to develop when I started in leadership was to look someone in the eyes. I found that to be incredibly awkward. What I quickly learned was one of the factors of being a great leader is to *make eye contact* with your team when speaking to them. What I found was that eye contact made my team feel important as well. They felt respected by me. When you are making eye contact with someone, you are telling them that you are speaking directly to them, and you want them to know that it's important. *Eye contact establishes a non-verbal connection with your team member.* Eye contact is a sign of confidence as a leader. People feel honored when you are making eye contact with them.

When your eyes aren't on the person you are talking to, you are telling them a few things. First, what you have to say must not be that important if you're not even looking at me. Second, who you are saying it to must not matter too much to get your attention. Three, what you are doing is more important than who is in the room with you. Clearly, none of those items are good. This may not even be your intention, but it is your message. Everyone judges others by the action but want to be judged by their intent. Let's make both of them align.

The Best is Yet to Come…Right?

Lastly, what I want to share with you is incredibly important. I purposefully waited to share this one last because it's one of the more important elements of being a great communicator. In order for you to be a great communicator, you must *believe in what you are saying…or don't say it at all.* Your team, regardless of how highly you think of them, is even smarter than you think. People can sniff out dubious people and dubious messages at an impressive rate. By communicating a message to your team, you don't believe in, you're telling them that your vision or mission is uncertain. You can't possibly ask your organization to get behind you and where you're taking them, if you don't even believe the words coming out of your mouth. Great leaders are confident and convinced that what they are saying is real, and the right thing to say. *When communicating with your team, you must have unshakable truth married to an unshakable confidence. Being a great leader requires you to be a great communicator.*

Characteristic #3

When my youngest daughter Brooklyn was a toddler, she had to know where we were going, any time we hopped in the car. Brooklyn could be in the middle of a conversation with her sister Deja and completely come to a halt, just to ask where we were going. Although, as you could imagine, those aren't the most fun times in the car with her, knowing where you're going matters. For anyone to be considered a great leader, they have to be a *visionary*. If a leader in any organization, doesn't have a vision for *where* they are going, their team will not be engaged. Period. *Engagement comes from a clear vision*. But is knowing *where* you're going enough? If so, then we can end the chapter right here. I think you and I both know, just knowing *where* you want to go won't suffice.

Why

Knowing where you want to go is only one battle in the large war. In order for a great leader to be considered a *visionary*, there are several other battles within the war we need to win. Another battle we face is knowing *why* we want to go there. As so many great leaders before me have said time and time again, people buy-in to the *why*. Stories, missions and visions, all become better and more contagious when we know the *why*. The *why* allows us to commit. Our mind and spirit want to be involved in what our bodies are committing to. It allows us to have an intimate connection to what we do. Knowing the *why* is not only great to establish an intimate connection, it is also great for attrition. *People commit to vision.* When you have a vision people can get behind, they don't want to leave. They use phrases like; "I love what I do". You can't put a value on an employee who loves what they do. They are committed, they work hard, their energy is contagious. That's what you want in your organization.

How(s)

The *visionary* establishes the what, the *why* establishes the commitment, so in order to keep this momentum going, we need the *how*. This *how* isn't singular, it's plural. Every great leader must establish two different types of *how*. The first *how* we are going to discuss is; *how are we going to get there*? There is nothing worse than a leader who casts the vision, talks about the why and when it comes time to talk about the *how*, they're silent. This is a pivotal point for a leader and their vision. This is where you can lose all confidence. You lose confidence not only in yourself, but your team loses it in you.

Every vision should be broken down into the most segmented details you possibly can. Doing so will help you identify potential obstacles and how to overcome them. More importantly, when the questions are raised by your team (and believe me, they will be), you are ready to respond with confidence. When you find your vision, before communicating it out, break it down. You can do this a number of different ways. There is no one-way to do this. I like to think of this like project management. I find my vision, I break it down into sections by dividing my mission statement into topical categories. Then I have a bullet point break down under each category. When I do this, I can identify the why quickly and identify the potential obstacles clearly. Once you are able to do this, you will have no problem finding your *how*.

The other *how* I want to talk about is just as important as the first one. As a great leader, communicating *how* your team plays a part in the overall vision, will solidify your team's commitment. We know the vision, great! We know why you want to do it, awesome! We even know how you're going to get there, incredible! But, where the heck do I fit in? This is actually one of my favorite questions from my team members. This enables me to pour out the love and appreciation I have for each of them, by acknowledging all they do and *how* it directly relates to the success of the organization.

When you take the time to explain to your team *how* they play a role in the big vision (and you should be doing this without being prompted by the question), you become their favorite leader. I could wait my whole life and you would not be able to identify one person who doesn't want to feel appreciated and be told how they belong to something bigger than them. It just won't happen. We were all designed to be a part of something greater than us. If we are going to ask people to give us 40+ hours a week of their time away from their friends and family, we should at minimum, be able to tell them how much we appreciate them. We should, at minimum, be able to tell them *how* they bless us and play a part in the overall success of the organization. That is what great leaders do for their teams.

Keep It Fresh

Ok, we have established that we need to be a *visionary*. We have established that we need to know our *why*. We have established that we need to identify our *how*(s). The next course of action a great leader does as a *visionary* is *keeping the vision fresh in our own mind, as well as the minds of the team*. If you're married, picture this scenario in your home. Your wedding day comes; you tell your spouse that you love them. A year has gone by and you haven't told them you love them since your wedding day. One afternoon, your spouse walks up to you and says, "Babe, I haven't heard you tell me you love me since our wedding day." You respond with, "You know I love you. If anything changes, I will let you know." Needless to say, you're about to have a bad day. The same is true with you sharing your vision with your team. *At minimum, you should be communicating your vision every*

30 days. This allows for you to be reminded on why you're doing what you're doing, in the middle of all the busyness that comes with your role as a leader. This also keeps the vision fresh in your team's mind. Everyone plays a role, as we already established. Sometimes that role becomes redundant or doesn't give you a chance to breathe. It is in those times we remind ourselves of the vision. If it has been too long since you or they have heard it, it could become a little less clear and hard to remind ourselves.

I recently read a report that said only 7% of today's employees know their company's business strategies, and what's expected of them. An easy way to solve this organizational nightmare is by communicating your vision, why you're doing it and how you're going to get there…EVERY 30 DAYS. There is no excuse for there to only be 7% of employees knowing what is expected of them and the company's business strategy. This falls solely on leadership. If you can honestly say you communicate your vision on a regular basis (once a month), you can confidently say your team knows what is expected of them. As leaders, we owe it to our team to keep them feeling a part of the big picture.

The way I like to stay in control of this, again, is by breaking it down. I communicate daily objectives, weekly goals, a monthly vision and a quarterly recap of how we did. Annually, we celebrate the successes of the year. In all this, we acknowledge people for their hard work and contribution. We celebrate people. This keeps your team energized and excited to keep going! A paycheck isn't going to do it. Your team can get a paycheck anywhere, but they may be hard-pressed to find a leader.

What's the Plan Man?!

When leading a team and going after your vision, a leader has to be *strategic*. There have been quite a few catastrophic errors made over the years, by leaders, for lack of strategy. The decisions we make as leaders should be done with precision and purpose. *Decisions made on the fly, generally lead to by-chance results.* One thing we have to be comfortable with is making the decision that's the best overall for the organization. Sometimes we are forced to make decisions that aren't always popular, but as long as they're what is best, you are making the right decision.

Leadership is a tall order. Leaders are placed in tough situations. Without these developed characteristics we have discussed so far, your experience as a leader is going to be unsuccessful. The decisions we make shouldn't be a surprise for us, if we have broken down the vision for the organization. You should've anticipated the obstacle. You should've anticipated the challenge. That is the premise behind breaking your goal down. When we do this, we avoid knee-jerk reactions, and implement incremental changes to adapt. When a ship wants to turn, it doesn't yank the helm, it makes incremental shifts that will inevitably point them to their destination. Leadership is a large ship, making constant turns to reach its destination.

Characteristic #4

Close your eyes and imagine this scenario. A young, single-mom comes to work every day on time. She's one of your best employees, a real team-player. She has a stellar attitude, great work-ethic, knows her job function better than you've seen in a long time. Today, in the office, you have a big project to get started on. This employee of yours plays a key role in the success of this project, but remember, it's just the beginning. All of a sudden, your key employee gets a phone call from her daycare that says, "Your son is sick, he needs to be picked up from daycare and taken to the urgent care. He's running a pretty high fever." This world-class employee of yours says, "I have to go. My son is sick. I need to take him to the urgent care." What do you do? This is clearly rhetorical but let me tell you what I experienced at an office one morning.

The boss of this employee allowed her to leave and when she walked out the door, she said, "I need robots, not single-moms. Remind me never to hire a single-mom." I know, disgusting, but it's a true story. One of most tangible characteristics that make a great leader is one who can be *compassionate*. There are some people in positions of authority, that are viewed as leaders, who are incredibly insufficient in this area. Too many times we see people confuse being *compassionate* with tolerating behavior. If the story I stated was a common situation for that team member, then yes, letting her leave without some sort of disciplinary action would be tolerance. But remember, this is a hard-working, team-oriented, talented individual. Clearly, this is someone who doesn't do this on a regular basis. Being *compassionate* allows your team to see the human-side of their leader. Now, compassion won't always be scenario specific. A lot of times, you will find being *compassionate* as simply being a normal human-being with normal feelings.

What Do They Know About You?

There's a stigma when it comes to leaders getting to know their own team. What we are seeing are leaders fearing they'll lose their influence if they open-up to a team member. Or, leaders exposing too much of their insecurities, thus being judged on their ability to lead any further. Both fears are valid, and wrong. Let me explain. Like a person craving their favorite decadent dessert, it's all good in moderation. Getting to know your team is remarkably effective. How much more influential would you be to your team, if you simply asked them how their children are doing, by name? How much more respect would you gain from your team, if you asked them how their mother's chemotherapy is going? It is simple acts of compassion, or the state of being *compassionate*, that will help you become a great leader. Now, in regard to you being open with your team, I believe this should be done with caution. There are several reasons why, that I would like to share with you. Anytime you work with people, there will be a mess. Some people have ill-intent. They are fishing for information about you, just to justify their dislike for you. As negative and scandalous as that sounds, it's valid. This, unfortunately, is just how some people are. Of course, this does not speak for the majority. But as a leader, you want to protect your influence with your team. Being vulnerable, to a certain degree, can be monumental in your leadership. Opening-up too much can cripple it. I won't list out the do's and don'ts of what to say to your team. I want you to discern that on your own. You, and only you, know your team best.

Business as Usual

In a typical position within an organization, you spend 1/3 of your day in the office with your colleagues. You are spending valuable time away from your family and investing your time into the vision and mission of an organization. Naturally, spending that much time with a group of people, you want to just have a regular conversation that doesn't revolve around the organization. This is especially "cool" when you get to talk to your leader about something other than business. As leaders, we need to remind ourselves that we are leading people. People crave relationships. If all you talk about with your team as the leader is business, you aren't relatable to them. You are barely even human! You don't want to waste precious time talking about your favorite sports team for 2 hours of the day, but you do want to let them know that you do think about something other than the four walls you're in.

No One is a Mind-Reader

Part of being a great leader is being great at *compassion*. Part of being great at *compassion*, is expressing your appreciation for the team. *People leave leaders, not organizations*. I'm sure you have heard that a million times, and there was a million and one. If more leaders would grasp that, there would be less attrition in the marketplace. People want to feel appreciated. If I was investing 40+ hours a week to your vision, your mission and your organization, I want to (at minimum) feel appreciated. I have met countless people who have left jobs for less money, just to work for a better leader. I have also seen people turn down more money, just to stay with a great leader. How you treat people matters. The words you use (or don't use) matters. I have been in organizations where people go home crying, all because they can't stand the person they work for. If you are going to ever be a great leader, this should never happen. *Leaders love the team they have, and they love them enough to show it to them. This is the call of compassion for every great leader, love your team and build them up.*

Characteristic #5

One of the many great things I love about collegiate football is the anti-celebration after a touchdown. You actually receive a penalty flag for excessive celebration when you prolong or delay the game, because you want to rub it in that you just scored. It is a great lesson for the players that humility is more important than making this moment about you as an individual player. In order for anyone to be a great leader, they must be *humble*. Humility is an attractive quality in a leader. *Humility is a big-picture mentality that every leader should possess.*

I remember being at an event where the speaker on the stage made a comment that was a little edgy for the atmosphere they were in. After making the comment, the audience sort of reacted with an "oooohhh" noise, indicating that the comment was a little rough. The speaker then proceeded to say, "Oh calm down. But hey, I have the mic, so I can say that." Now, in fairness, I am going to assume they were joking on their ability to say what they want because they possess the microphone. On the other hand, this person was a leader. I will be honest, it left a very bad taste in mouth. I cringed when I heard them say that. The lack of humility in that moment was a missed opportunity for that leader. *Sometimes over talking can lead to a moment of insufficiency.* Humility (not insecurity) is a key component to becoming a great leader.

#Others

We live in a time where everyone is "me-focused". We have places designed to make us the center-focus of attention. Social media has something called a "selfie". A "selfie" is when you turn the camera of your phone away from world and point it at yourself, to take a picture. This has become such a phenomenon that we installed a front-facing camera, because we'd hate to make you have to turn your phone around. On top of that, we created an accessory you can attach to your phone, so you can grip it perfectly, to take the premier "selfie" with stability. We created "hashtags" (which is just the pound sign for us old people), to use as a search method to find a "#selfie". This brings up literally millions of "selfies". The "selfie" craze has become so important people will stop walking in front of you, just to take the ultimate timed "selfie". People even do this when they are driving.

If "selfies" weren't enough, social media has created a platform for you to share a video of your opinion about something that has nothing to do with you. You may be reading this and cracking up (as I am writing it), but it really is a day and age of "self". I have absolutely nothing against social media or selfies. However, I wanted to be clear about just how "me" focused we are. Great leaders are not "me" focused, they are "others" focused. Focusing on others allows you to do things for a greater cause. Focusing on others reminds you that every decision you make is bigger than you. *Focusing on others helps us to see the importance of the team we have and the people we get to do this life with.* Leadership is bigger than the office we work in. Being a great leader is being a great mother or father, a great friend or family member. Yes, we want to be great leaders in the marketplace, but that's not what leadership is all about. Focus on others and watch your life value increase exponentially.

Not Just What, But Where

In every great leaders' life, you will experience a moment when you have to discipline someone within your organization. This is never a fun time and it is never comfortable. Because discipline requires swift action (don't delay the discipline), it can sometimes be done in the worst way possible. When it comes to disciplining someone, a lot happens in a short amount of time. Leaders feel things like disappointment, anger, embarrassment and frustration. If we aren't careful, we can lose control of any one of these. What you say in these moments matter.

However, it's not just what you say in these moments that matter, but where you say it. *There is a rule of thumb I try and teach every leader I work with; praise publicly, discipline privately*. One of the greatest acts of humility is pulling your team member aside and disciplining them privately. This little step can change everything for that individual, your team and you as a leader. Could you imagine someone calling you out on your flaws in front of everyone? What feelings would be going through you? How would you respond? How would you feel about that individual who did that to you? This is exactly what is going through your team members mind when you discipline them publicly.

The arrogance of calling someone out in front of everyone is through the roof. If you love your team, respect your team, value your team and want to keep your team, discipline privately. When you choose to do the opposite, a few things happen. First, you now have an employee who feels incredibly disrespected, and should feel that way. Secondly, your viewers (the rest of your team) could potentially lose respect for that individual. They could potentially lose trust in that individuals' ability to contribute to the team, causing a massive separation. Thirdly, your team now fears you. This is not a compliment or an accomplishment. This is a flaw. Your team should never fear their leader. Fear is a power tool, not a *positive* influence tool. *Remember, great leaders have positive influence.*

Now, with the reverse effect, comes praising publicly. Chances are that when you had to discipline someone, the team knows they were disciplined. The error or mistake was most likely not a surprise to the rest of the team. The beautiful thing about this moment is that no one saw you discipline them. What this means for you, the disciplined team member and the rest of your team, is that everything can be re-established. Your team member didn't lose their self-respect and dignity, the team didn't lose trust in that team member, and you didn't become a fearful dictator. At the same time, you didn't lose respect for your team by not addressing the issue. There are so many wins in this situation.

Moving forward, when that team member does well (and they will because they want to try harder for you), take the time to stop and praise that person publicly. By doing this, you are publicly saying, "I love this person. I trust this person. I appreciate this person. I believe in this person and I want you all to do the same." This is nothing new to you and the team member, because you should have said this to them when you were disciplining them. But, this confirms it with the rest of the team. This little step of praising publicly is a big wave of cohesiveness and continuity.

Take and Give

Your wins or successes as a leader are collaborative. You don't win on your own, just like you don't lose on your own. However, if you want to be a great leader, you must be willing to *take the blame and give the credit*. Great leaders stand up and face the blame, as if it were all theirs. In the same way, great leaders stand up and acknowledge the collaborative effort with their team on any success, to the public. As a leader, we should never take the credit for the wins. Only for the losses. Whether a team succeeds or fails, falls on the ability of the leader. LeBron James is arguably the greatest basketball player to ever live (if you ever visited a barbershop, you've heard this argument). In 2015, LeBron James took a banged-up Cleveland Cavaliers team to the NBA Finals against an incredible Golden State Warriors basketball team.

Unfortunately, for the Cleveland Cavaliers, they did not win the championship that year. However, on every single interview I watched, LeBron James took the blame for the loss and gave the Golden State Warriors the credit for a great victory. Whether you love LeBron James as I do, or not, LeBron James showed incredible leadership. This is just one of many examples history has shown us of what a great leader looks like in the moments of failure (or success). Leaders don't take credit, they give it. Leaders don't give blame, they take it.

Characteristic #6

Great leaders are strong and courageous. They don't have to be fearless, just courageous. *Fearlessness is the absence of fear; I don't believe that is achievable. Courageousness is doing what is right; while standing in the face of fear.* When it comes to being a great leader, one must be able to be *courageous*. Courage is the difference between internally *feeling* something and *externally* doing something. Courage separates the men from the boys, the women from the girls. Courage is fortitude in action!

I Believe! I Believe! I Believe!

A major part of being a great leader is in the mind. Great leaders don't just say they can achieve their goals, they *believe* it! Belief is a change-agent for a leader. Leaders who believe in themselves have the courage to stand-up for what is right and reject what is wrong. Leaders who believe in themselves don't sway back and forth on their values and principles. Leaders who believe in themselves have the courage (or a pessimist might call the naivety) to believe in their team as well. There are countless stories of leaders who couldn't relinquish control of responsibilities because they didn't have the courage to believe in themselves as a leader, or their team's ability to perform. Believing in yourself, your team and the unbelievable, blows the door of doubt off and erases fearfulness. Believing in yourself is a component of expectation for the unbelievable. Belief doesn't make you fearless, but it does make you fear-less.

No, Not Now, No Thank You

Being courageous isn't without its flaws when misused. Because being courageous allows us to believe in the unbelievable, it also leads us to do the unnecessary. Great leaders are passionate about what they do. Great leaders have compassion for others. Great leaders want to see others do great. This sometimes leads to great leaders over-extending themselves, eliminating room for what's important like friends and family. Great leaders master the art of saying *no*. Although leaders want to be able to help everyone succeed, we simply can't do it all. Learning how to say *no* as a leader creates healthy boundaries for you.

In order for great leaders to say *no*, it is going to take some courage. Saying *no* as a leader is key to having a healthy marriage, friendships and overall physical health. Over-extending yourself as a leader can cause many problems in your personal life. Leaders have to set boundaries by using the word *no*. People love you, they love how you inspire them, and they want to be around great leaders. This is a tremendous compliment to you. But, these same people don't have limits on how much time they want of yours. They will take every minute they can get if they could. The people that *want* your time tend to forget other people that *need* your time. This isn't because they're selfish or blood-sucking time jacker's, it's because they truly admire you. If you're anything like me, you want to help everyone you can. But, to be a great leader, you have to learn how to say *no*.

Don't Reject the Life Vest

There's an old story of a man swimming in the Pacific, when the tide took him out a little too far. He prayed, "LORD, please help me...I'm drowning." About 1 minute later a man came on a boat. He offered the gentleman a life vest, he respectfully rejected. He said, "No thank you, God is going to save me." Another minute went by, and another boat came with a life vest. Again, the drowning man said, "No thank you, God is going to save me." After about 3 minutes, another boat came. The man in the boat said, "Sir, I have a life vest for you, put it on!" The man replied, "NO! GOD IS GOING TO SAVE ME!" Just a short while later, the man died in the Pacific Ocean. When he went to heaven, he asked God, "LORD, why didn't you save me?" God replied, "I tried to save you. I sent you three boats."

In order for you to be a great leader, you have to learn how to *accept help*. There are several reasons why a leader doesn't *accept help*. The first reason, and it's the real reason why all leaders don't *accept help*, is because they just don't know they need it. I find this a lot in young leaders. When I say young leaders, I mean leaders who are new to leadership. A young leader has a quality that is great when it comes to vision, but terrible when it comes to strategy. That quality is naivety. Some of the more experienced leaders have been jaded by disappointment and unsuccessful attempts at something they were incredibly passionate about. These experiences have made them self-proclaimed "realists". When in reality, they simply fear another unsuccessful attempt. Young leaders embrace the challenge and will "swing for the fence" with their vision. I personally love this about young leaders!

However, here is where the problem lies with that, when it comes to strategy. When being strategic, it takes help. Strategy takes a team of people that range in experience and expertise. Young leaders will view a challenging vision as an opportunity to prove themselves and will disregard help. This can bury you as a leader. No one wants to work with or for someone who can't get past themselves and ask for help. Remember, being a leader means that someone is trusting and following you. Be respectful enough not to lead them right into a brick wall.

You will find that more experienced leaders will be able to identify your areas of risk faster than you. If they are great leaders, they will offer you some advice. Advice is a healthy suggestion to keep you on track, moving forward and minimizing risk. Don't confuse this with the naysayers that will suggest something can't be done, because they weren't able to do it. There is a big difference between advice and doubt. Time will allow you to become better at deciphering between the two; but be willing to *accept help*. Great leaders are knowledgeable enough to know that life requires help. Great leaders are also vulnerable enough to *accept help*.

Lose the Popular Vote

One of the elements of being *courageous* is *standing for what is right*. How many times can you recount hearing a President run on one idea, and completely U-turn to the popular idea when elected? Now, this isn't about politics, as much as it is being a great leader and *standing for what is right*. *Great leaders aren't looking for the popular vote*. Great leaders are looking to establish the right way to run their organization. Great leaders don't care about what others think is the right thing to do. Not many will understand your vision. God didn't give them the vision, He gave it to you! As a great leader, you have to dig deep and stand your ground when it comes to doing what is right for you and your organization.

Everyone Already Knows

Anytime a leader is wrong, it's generally no surprise to everyone else. *Success moves like molasses but failure travels fast*. When a leader is wrong, people are quick to talk about it. Everyone has the perfect answer to your problem. Everyone knows exactly what they would've done if they were in your shoes. Everyone becomes subject matter experts, post failure. In stating all that, delaying the truth that you were wrong only deteriorates your leadership. Great leaders move swiftly to say, *"I was wrong"*, and move on. Delaying what everyone else already knows is simply your pride and ego at work. Great leaders admit their mistakes. They own them and move past them. The faster you accept it, the faster you can move past it. This level of transparency takes courage. *In order for you to be a great leader, you must be courageous!*

Characteristic #7

On May 2nd, 2011, President Barack Obama was informed of the whereabouts of terrorist, Osama Bin Laden. Because of the time sensitivity of the matter, President Obama had to make a swift decision, capture or wait for another opportunity. It was in that moment that President Barack Obama exemplified great leadership. On May 2nd, 2011, the U.S. Navy SEALS eliminated their target, Osama Bin Laden. In order for you to be a great leader, you must learn to be *decisive*.

Swift Doesn't Always Mean Smart

It's tough to sit in the hot seat as a leader and have to make a swift decision. Great leaders cannot live by ready…fire…aim, our decisions have to show *rationale. Great leaders make rational decisions*. When a leader takes the time to be rational in their decision-making, they can feel confident in the decision they've made. *Shooting from the hip* is irresponsible and reckless, when it comes to leadership.

Our decisions have wide-spread impact. We should make them with clarity and discernment. How we make decisions has a lasting impact on the climate of our organization and the influence in our leadership. You build (and lose) trust within your team on the decisions you make as a leader. Over the last decade, we have seen fast-growing start-ups nearly collapse on the poor decision-making from their leaders. Being *decisive* isn't about being able to make a quick decision, being *decisive* is about being able to make a *rational* decision.

See-Through Leadership

One of the greatest things you can do for your influence is to be *transparent*. Again, I remind you that leadership is bigger than you. Significantly. Having rationale behind our decisions allows us to be confident in the decisions we make. Being *transparent* in our decisions allows us to feel we are being fair in the decisions we make. Being open with your organizations about the decisions you make as the leader, allows them to feel as if they were a part of the process. There are no surprises or unforeseen circumstances when we are *transparent* in our decision-making. *Transparency* doesn't mean sending an email out to the entire organization when you decide to purchase a new software for a particular department. Things like that should be on a "need to know" basis.

What *transparency* does look like however is no "surprise" layoffs, no "stores closing" email the month before it does, no "we've committed to moving our call-center hours to 24 hours a day" starting next week. These types of knee-jerk decisions create a toxic environment and cause massive hemorrhaging in your bottom line. If you think "hiding" crucial decisions like this, that impact the lives of the people in your organization somehow help you save face for your company as a whole, you're fooling only yourself. Great leaders do what is right by being *transparent* in the decision-making. Decisions similar to the one's I listed above shouldn't be a surprise.

Wisdom > Emotion

Can you recall a time you made a decision you regret out of emotion and not wisdom? If you're a human being, of course you can! Welcome to the club, your certificate is in the mail. But seriously, emotionally-driven decisions are nothing new to leadership. Decisions like this, generally, never lead to the outcome we desired. *Great leaders learn how to make decisions out of wisdom and not emotion.* Since most of our decisions have a major impact to our team, there are a few guiding principles we need to exercise when being decisive.

The first principle is to *pause*. Pausing allows us to slow down the world around us. Remember that their urgency is not your urgency. You don't have to make a decision because someone else wants it now. Take the time to simply pause, before you make up your mind. Secondly, *gather the facts and assess*. As a great leader, never make a high-impact decision with little information. Again, being decisive isn't about making a quick decision, it's about making an informed decision. A decision that is based on wisdom and not emotion. Thirdly, *make sure your decision is best for the organization and not the individual.* What I want to caution you on is making a decision that impacts the team, without first assessing if it is best for the team. Lastly, *don't apologize to anyone for your decision.* This one, in my opinion, is critical. When you make a decision that you paused to think about, gathered information on and made sure it was best for the team, you don't have to worry about the impact. Don't apologize if someone doesn't agree with you. *Everyone is not going to agree with you as a leader.* That's ok! You aren't looking for the popular vote. *You are looking to be decisive, as a great leader should be.*

Characteristic #8

My favorite college football team on this entire planet is the University of Washington Huskies (Go Dawgs). One of my favorite stories from this team is Jake Locker. Jake Locker was the starting Quarterback for UW from 2007 – 2010. In 2011, Jake Locker was the number eight pick in the NFL Draft for the *Tennessee Titans*. Four years later, Jake announced he was done with football. Jake stated he lacked a "burning desire" to play the game. You might read that story and think, "why in the world is that one of his favorites?" That's fair, but you are missing the leadership lesson in that. Jake Locker knew what he didn't want to do any longer. In order for you to be a great leader, you must be *passionate* about what you do.

Search Deep

Many people wondered why Jake Locker all of a sudden walked away from football? Some even wondered how he could walk away from all that money? The reason why Jake was able to do so is because he lacked the passion for it any longer, or in his words, the "burning desire". Jake was the offensive captain on his team. He was the leader in that huddle. Jake knew, subconsciously, to be a great leader you have to be *passionate* about what you do. Jake had the respect for his team to say, "I'm done", instead of carrying on knowing he wasn't giving all he had due to his lack of passion. I could only imagine the ridicule and judgment he faced, knowing he walked away from a childhood dream. Jake didn't listen to the outside noise, he listened to his own mind and made a decision best suitable for the organization as a whole. That is great leadership at its finest! Ask yourself, "Do I have a deep desire to do what I do?" If the answer to that question is *no*, I urge you to reconsider being the leader. It's not fair to you, your team, your family or your future.

Commitment

When you become the Captain of a ship, you sign (figuratively) an agreement saying you will not 'abandon ship' while passengers are still on. This is a longtime maritime tradition and honor. This honor says that you are committed to what you do and who you do it for. This level of commitment can only come from a great leader who is passionate about what they do. Could you imagine being on a ship with anyone who is less than a great leader at the helm? I certainly wouldn't want to be. *In order for you to be a great leader, you have to be committed to what you do, and who you do it for.* Great leaders understand the big picture. Who is involved? How important are they to me? Where is my leadership taking them?

For servants like Captains, is my decision-making leading them to their death? These are real decisions, made by real people, who are great leaders. Great leadership requires a great commitment to the work and the people.

Are You Motivated?

Every morning in my house, it is a process to wake-up my kids. I have yet to see them spring out of bed, full of joy, ready to take on the day (unless it's Christmas or we are going on vacation). My kids moan and groan, they drag their feet, they whine and complain, they even fall back asleep! Clearly, my kids lack motivation to live life in the morning. I really can't say I'm any different. I am just not a morning person.

However, when it comes to leadership, I don't need any motivation. I love speaking about leadership, teaching about leadership, and of course, being a leader. I can do that all day. I can be a leader in the morning, I can be a leader when I'm tired, I can be a leader when I'm sick, I love leadership. I simply do not need motivation to be a leader and neither should you. *In order to be a great leader, you have to be self-motivated.* No one should have to motivate you to lead your team. This is your team, your responsibility and people are trusting you to take them somewhere. *Great leaders are not afforded the luxury of a bad day.* We don't have the right to be un-motivated. We took on the role of leadership and we are responsible for staying motivated.

Motivation Reflects Leadership

Being a great leader is a daunting task, but being anything but great in your leadership is a waste of time. Don't underestimate your influence with the people on your team. I remember working for an organization where the people in positions of authority walked around talking about how much they hated their jobs, being in the office and how much they wanted to leave. They lacked motivation more than I have ever seen.

These same people in positions of authority complained about their team's unwillingness to help out, their "it's not my job" attitude, their constant late arrivals to work, but could not understand where it stemmed from. As a great leader, to avoid this climate in your organization, you have to ask yourself a serious question. The question is, "If the rest of my team shared my passion, would I be happy with that?" Your passion leaks. Your team is watching you. Your team is mimicking you. Who else should they watch? If you fear, they fear. If you're angry, they're angry. If you lack motivation, they lack motivation. Every great leader can confidently say, "my level of passion is acceptable for my team."

Characteristic #9

Henry Ford said, "If everyone is moving forward together, then success takes care of itself." If you've never heard of Henry Ford, you've definitely seen his product. Henry Ford is the Founder of *Ford Motor Company*. The most successful motor company in the world. Needless to say, he knew a thing or two about how to be successful. In order for you to be a great leader, you have to be *collaborative*. Collaboration is the piston to the engine, the wheel to the tire or the gas to the vehicle. In other words, you aren't going anywhere if you aren't collaborating with other parts. As we discovered earlier, we need each other to be successful. A good indicator that an organization or team is successful is if they're *collaborative*.

Connect

In order for you to bring collaboration amongst your team, *you have to know your team members. No one should know your team better than you.* That's so nice, I'm going to say it twice. *No one should know your team better than you.* Great leaders spend time getting to know their team and their strengths. If you are unfamiliar with what your team is good at, you can't possibly be leading them well. Knowing your team and their strengths allows you to connect the right team members together, to achieve the greatest level of a common good. If your team has a big presentation to the Board of Directors, you don't put two analytical people together who are poor presenters. You wouldn't put two visionaries together, they would never get anything done. Connecting your team members to their strengths create the optimal level of production.

Emulsifier

One of my favorite people on the planet is my great friend Eric Boles. Eric Boles is the President and Founder of The Game Changers Inc. He is a leader of leaders. He is also an incredible communicator. I had the fortunate opportunity to attend an event he was speaking at when he brought up the idea of emulsification. Eric said that egg is the emulsifier in mayonnaise. As we all know from our 6th grade science class, oil and vinegar don't mix. However, when you add egg to the equation, the two substances that once couldn't be in the same jar together, are now working together to create the great product we all know as mayonnaise.

What Eric was trying to tell us was that leaders (or on that day Jesus) are great emulsifiers. *Great leaders are great emulsifiers.* Great leaders know how to bring two opposites together, to create a positive, productive team. Being an emulsifier allows you to hire strategically, bring together confidently and collaborate effectively. The difference between being an emulsifier or not, is to be confident in the success of your team.

Actions Speak Louder than Words

The best way to get your team to be collaborative is to show them how it's done. In July of 2018, coffee tycoons *Starbucks* and *McDonalds* announced a collaborative effort on a new campaign called the *NexGen Cup Challenge*. This initiative is designed to create a fully compostable, recyclable cup that would help reduce pollution and eliminate the use of plastic straws altogether. What Kevin Johnson and Steve Easterbrook did was show great leadership, collaborative leadership at a level higher than most of us could reach. This collaborative effort did more than just create an initiative to reduce waste, it showed both organizations that even with your competitor, you can be collaborative for a greater cause.

The impact this will have on their teams and organizations, as a whole, will be for years to come. They witnessed two major organizations come together to create a product that will impact the world. I hope you can understand the powerful image that does for their teams. Watching your leader work collaboratively does something almost magical to your thought process. This image says that it is bigger than me, it is even bigger than our organization, this is about making the greatest impact possible. *Great leaders are great exemplifiers of collaboration.*

Let It Go

Part of creating a culture of collaboration is being able to trust your team to get it done. What that means is once you've built the team that's going to work together, set the expectations (the sail) and let the team go. In the early phases of learning to promote collaboration, leaders tend to start off well, but then micro-manage the team. This is counter-productive to the idea of collaboration. Trust your team that they can get the job done. More importantly, trust yourself as a leader that you put the best team possible together. *Great leaders trust their team to perform.* If not, why did you hire them? The great Steve Jobs said, "It doesn't make sense to hire smart people and then tell them what to do, we hire smart people so they can tell us what to do."

I do want to be thorough in what that looks like, or doesn't look like. This doesn't mean you put together a team and walk away from the project or objective altogether. This means you trust them to get it done, and check-in on the progress of the goal. Allow your team the flexibility and space to be creative. Magic happens when you put a team together of complementary strengths. You get to see their best in action. Don't suffocate or block that from happening, because you can't be a collaborative leader.

Characteristic #10

Great leaders have mastered the art of having difficult conversations. Notice I didn't say great leaders have mastered the art of difficult conversations, I simply said of having them. *In order for you to be a great leader, you must be honest.* To have a difficult conversation with a team member about performance, attitude or overall contribution to the team, doesn't mean it has to be negative. It does however have to be *honest.* The longer you wait to address a problem on your team, the bigger and more contagious the problem becomes. Avoid the delay at all costs. No matter how many times you have a difficult conversation with a team member, it will never get comfortable. As a leader, you have to be comfortable being uncomfortable.

The Truth Doesn't have to Hurt

We have seen it before. The leader pulls an under-performing team member in their office and they circumvent the difficult conversation. They begin to tip-toe around the actual problem or the "elephant in the room". Instead, they find a soft way to say there is a problem, but I do not want to actually say what it is. Then what happens is the team member leaves the office confused. They go back out into the workplace and continue to under-perform, until you (the leader) or the employee are let go. You create a culture of mediocrity and less than stellar effort within your organization. All of this can be avoided by being *honest* with your team about what your expectations are of them. Remember, we are not going for the popular vote. *Great leaders are honest about where their team members are and where they need to be.*

When you are delivering difficult news, don't sugarcoat it. At the same time, don't uppercut your team either. How we deliver difficult news, as leaders, is all about balance. Keep in mind that you hired this person because you saw something great in them. Inside every person on your team is a *champ* and a *chump*. Whatever you speak to inside them is going to come out. Great leaders bring the best out of people, even in the middle of a difficult conversation, through *honesty*. *Honesty* opens the door for genuine conversation, vulnerability and causes break-through to happen for you and the team member. Society has created a *culture of offense.*

Everyone is offended by the truth now. If you tell an employee they are under-performing to the expectations of the position they hold, they're offended. If you ask an employee to step-it-up, they feel offended by your lack of appreciation for their current efforts. Great leaders cannot worry about being offensive, they have to worry about being *honest*. You do nothing for the team member by circumventing an issue. Great leaders address the issue head-on. *You can completely avoid offense by being honest in your assessment, encouraging in your beliefs, respectful in your language, appreciative of them as people and clear in your expectations.* Anything outside of that is not of your concern or control.

The Square Burger

Fast-food restaurant *Wendy's* is famously known for their square burgers. The reason *Wendy's* decided to make their burgers square is for consumers to see the quality of the meat, and lastly, because they want us to know that *Wendy's* doesn't cut corners. *In order for you to be a great leader, you never cut corners. Great leaders do everything the way it should be done in their job.* Cutting corners in your work ethic shows. Your team sees it, your bottom-line sees it, your board sees it, even your dog sees it (kidding)! But seriously, it's a big deal to do your job correctly. You are the example for your team and when you have a work-ethic of cutting corners, so will your team.

At What Expense

Every organization has a fiscal year. Within that fiscal years comes quarterly goals, monthly objectives and weekly tasks, all to reach the desired result of the fiscal year. There's a lot of pressure on the leaders within an organization to reach those results. We think about the livelihood of our family, the embarrassment of falling short, the annual review we are going to have that will certainly mention our short-comings. With this level of pressure, we are going to have to decide to be *honest*. Every leader is given the opportunity to bend the rules at some point or another. Bending these rules will feel beneficial for you. It may even go un-noticed, but you never want to sacrifice honesty for production. We've seen organizations take nasty pitfalls because they simply weren't *honest. Production and numbers are important, but not at the expense of being honest.*

Characteristic #11

At the beginning of this book, I spoke about the *roots* of a great leader. Every great leader has the exact same *root*. No matter who you choose, anywhere in history, you will find one characteristic that is the exact same at the *root*. This characteristic is the foundation of all great leaders. Everything we do, every decision we make, every conversation we have starts with this characteristic. *In order for you to be a great leader, at the root, must be integrity.*

Dictionary.com defines *integrity* as; "adherence to moral and ethical principles; soundness of moral character; honesty." Integrity is the good "soil" of the tree that produces the "good fruit", or the 10 other characteristics of a great leader. When you are *rooted* in integrity as a leader, everything else falls into place. This entire book is worthless to you, if you don't get this principle down. This principle is the *alpha* and *omega* of every great leader. As we learned, every bad leadership decision we have ever seen or heard of was *rooted* in insufficiency. Well, every great leadership decision we have ever seen or heard of was *rooted* in *integrity*.

This is Where it Begins

Every great leader is faced with countless decisions on a day-to-day basis. Each decision we make has an impact on our organization. It would be wise to have a foundation to start from before making these decisions. This is a foundation that you are so deeply *rooted* in that you innately make decisions from this starting point. That *root* is *integrity*. When you make decisions from a *root* of *integrity*, you never have to worry about if it is the right decision. You are making a decision from moral and ethical principles. When you make a decision on behalf of your team or your organization from moral and ethical principles, they can be rest assured it's what's best for them. When your team knows their leader is *rooted* in *integrity*, the level of trust you build and the bond you create is unbreakable. *Everything a great leader does begins at integrity.*

Accountability

Great leaders hold themselves accountable to their teams. Knowing you have a team watching you, sometimes, won't be enough. However, knowing you have a team depending on you changes everything. Accountability is a "sticky product" for your team. When your team knows they have a leader that will be accountable to them, they never want to leave. *Your team lays anchor where they feel the water is the calmest.* Being accountable to your team creates a calmness over them. They can breathe and relax, knowing their leader isn't going to one day abandon ship. Every team needs a leader who is accountable to them. You are the one they are looking to for guidance and direction. Be there for your team. *In order for you to be a great leader, you have to be accountable to your team.*

Mirror Mirror on the Wall...

In the everyday hustle and bustle of leadership, we can lose sight of the person in the mirror. We are in a fast-paced, high-demand environment each and every day. This level of speed can sometimes get the best of us. *In order for you to maintain an appropriate level of integrity, you have to stop and do a self-audit to see what may need some adjusting. Integrity* isn't about getting it right all the time, it's about being willing and able to adjust it at any time. Great leaders take the time to self-evaluate and be honest with the person in the mirror about where they are in their leadership *integrity*. It is not only imperative to the success of your team, but also in the success of you as an individual. Your team needs you to self-audit to keep your organization on track. Take the time to hit the brakes and evaluate.

Who Do You Say That I Am?

When your team leaves work they spend time with their family and friends. In that time, they are asked about their jobs and their leaders. The answer they give those individuals is your true reputation with that person. The reason why leaders seldom get to hear that reputation is because their teams fear their response. It's hard to sit in the office of your leader and tell them how you honestly feel. What if I get fired? What if I get overlooked for the next promotion? What if I am treated differently moving forward? These are all very valid concerns. *Great leaders build a culture of constructive feedback.* Your team should be free (respectfully) to share their thoughts or opinions on your leadership, with you, without penalty for their feedback. Who you think you are, who they think you are, shouldn't differ much.

In order for you to be who you want to be, you have to know who they believe you are. If it doesn't align, adjust it. Ask questions like, "Why do you feel that way about me? How can I change your perception? What are 3 things I could change right now to get me moving in the right direction?" This type of freedom will build tremendous respect for you as a leader on your team. *Egos with your amigos is no bueno.* Your pride and ego will hinder you from ever becoming a great leader. They blind you from your dark-side. *Great leaders with integrity embrace feedback and use it to move the team forward.*

True North

Everyone has a moral compass. This is the internal direction in which your morals head you towards as a leader. Every man and woman must make the decision as to where their moral compass is going to point. With every single decision we make, we must first decide as to where our moral compass is going to point. It's the decision before the decision. When you operate in your leadership with your moral compass pointing at *true north*, you can feel at ease about yourself as a great leader. For me, I have principles I rely on for my moral compass in my leadership. I certainly don't always get it right, but it is my compass. I make mistakes in my leadership. I have my moments where I could have done better. But I truly believe that if your moral compass is set to *true north*, you will always return to a place of *integrity*.

In Conclusion

I once heard a leader say, "your misery is your ministry." When I heard that, I thought she was talking about something related to church. What she was really saying is that whatever drives you nuts the most, keeps you up at night and makes you want to scream, is probably the problem you should fix. For me, that *misery* is poor leadership. I created my curriculum, wrote this book and share this idea with anyone I could because I knew I was created to help develop great leaders. After reading this, you should see that this is no easy fix. In fact, this is the hardest thing I have ever had to do. In order for you to develop great leaders, you must first experience poor leadership, directly or indirectly.

Leadership is what's going to make our world a better place. It is going to take great leaders to stand-up against hatred, bigotry, racism, sexism, divisiveness and every other ugly behavior that stops our world from progressing. It takes great leadership to show the rest of the world what it takes to change it. My call-to-action for you is to embrace the leader inside you. Please don't ignore the calling of great leadership on life. You were strategically designed to impact the world, and someone is waiting for your leadership. I believe in the principles I've presented to you in this book. I believe with these *11 Characteristics of a Great Leader*, you can literally change the world. You have been called and challenged to impact the world. Are you ready to be a great leader?

PEAK CONSULTING

About the Author

Nelson J. Estrada is the Founder and President of *Peak Consulting.* Nelson is a highly-regarded leadership and executive consultant who has helped many different types of organizations grow and develop their leadership teams and cultures. From non-profits to multi-million dollar financial institutions, Nelson has equipped leaders with incredible principles that have helped their team's performance and establish a winning culture.

Nelson has served in various leadership roles throughout his career and has cultivated many relationships over the years. These core principles Nelson brings to your team can be applied across all levels of your organization; helping you grow your current core leaders, as well as developing new ones.